A LEG TO STAND ON

How to Live Without Excuses, Be Unstoppable, and Choose to Thrive After Losing a Limb

By

James R. Morey

A LEG TO STAND ON

How to Live Without Excuses,
Be Unstoppable, and Choose
to Thrive After Losing a Limb

Published by

Customer Strategy Academy, LLC
16212 Bothell Everett Hwy, Suite F111, Mill Creek, WA 98012
Publisher Jackie Morey's email: CustomerStrategyAcademy@gmail.com

Copyright Use and Public Information

ISBN: 978-1-7332501-9-1 Paperback

Limits of Liability and Disclaimer of Warranty

Disclaimer

DEDICATION

I consider myself a truly blessed and fortunate man, even with the challenges of an amputation.

I dedicate this book to my lovely, amazing, beautiful wife Jackie who is the most wonderful woman on earth. Jackie is, and has been, my Love, my Life and my best friend. Without her, I would never have written this book, nor done several other significant things, really.

I also dedicate this book to our two energetic and incredible children, Michael, and Alyssa. They are always a joy to us and fill our lives with entertainment, challenge, and love.

To our dearest friends Arthur and Sharon who went above and beyond, by sponsoring me to a couple of months of Personal Training after I got my permanent prosthetic leg – thank you very much! I dedicate this book to you.

To our loving and caring friend Rusti Brookes, who drove all the way from Idaho and stayed with us shortly after my surgery – to prepare meals, support us in whatever Jackie and I needed, and took the kids for walks and special trips – thank you very much! I dedicate this book to you.

I also dedicate this book to my Lord and Savior Jesus Christ, without Whom, I would not be here, nor would I have life, love, liberty, and hope. He has been with me throughout a life filled with challenges, heartaches, triumphs, and hard choices. He is my All.

ACKNOWLEDGEMENTS

I'd like to acknowledge the following friends and relatives for their deep love, thoughtfulness, care, lavish generosity, financial support, the prepared-and-delivered meals, supernatural prayers, emotional support, physical help, gift cards, and so much more.

Uncle Bob and Aunt Dolores Stead, Arthur and Sharon Best, Steve and Jacki Yust, Paul and Amy Weisz, Tom and Natalie Dyer, Tony and Rusti Brookes, Joyce De Guzman, Mark and Dawn Cundy, Moses and Lisa Sinclaire, Dick and Ruth Cinkovich, Van and Laurie Sperry, Pam Joy, Mark and Renee Oostra, Sean and Rona Allen, Jon and Aline Pinkston, Evelyn Prill, Kelly Hatfield, Tom and Sandy Quiring, Brian and Lisa Bate, Dr. Jessica Vera, Lorentz and Mary Lou Lorentzen, Col. Kevin Bushey (Ret.), Pamela Pollock, Uncle Nemsy and Tita Perla Gubatan, Uncle Vic and Tita Grace Torrijos, Stephen and Sherrie Brown, Rebekah

Blanton, Rolland Wright, Chad and Heather Collins, Rose Lorentzen, Michael and Janet Walker, James Heath, Michael and Vikki Byland, Jerin Bynum, Kenneth and Diane McIntyre, Gary and Dr. Becky Slabaugh, Margarita Naumchik, Mary Beth Woll, Victor Torrijos, Jr., Camille Alexander, Tong and Jen Pineda, Josh Pineda, Caleb Pineda, Matt and Gloria Buchanan, Pam Bennetsen, Cathy Dockter, Penny McGillivray, Norma Stryzewski, Gary and Sherri Larkin.

Thank you very much for all that you've invested into me and my family.

TABLE OF CONTENTS

INTRODUCTION

This is the story of a below the knee amputation (BKA) of my left leg. Most of the content is aimed at BKA and AKA amputees, but a good portion is also relevant to upper limb amputees, and family members.

But more importantly, this is more a story of challenge and hope, that is relevant to *everyone*.

This is a story of hope, not tragedy. It's a story of challenges not roadblocks. Molehills, not mountains.

It's my story, but it might also be *your* story.

Perhaps your story is about to start, has already started, or you're a pro. We share an experience, elements of a common story, and we can all learn from each other, gain strength from each other, be encouraged together.

Maybe you're *not* an amputee, but a family member, friend, or a caregiver – and you want some insight, hope, encouragement, or some advice from someone who *has* gone through it.

Whoever you are, whatever role you're playing in the story, or wherever in the story you are, I hope that you'll gain insight, understanding, hope, encouragement, and laugh a bit – because life is joyful, even if you, or a loved one, has been thrown a curveball.

My hope is that this book can help you to get your stance at the plate, keep your eye on that curveball, and knock that sucker out of the park!

CHAPTER 1

A CURVEBALL

Sometimes life throws us a curve ball.

You're late for work, and the car won't start. You need to do a presentation, your computer battery dies and you can't find the charge cord.

Some of these curve balls are temporary challenges.

Other curveballs are permanent, *life-changing* challenges. One of these happened to me on July 10th, 2020.

We were all ready to go on a family vacation to visit some dear friends in Idaho that we hadn't seen for years. I was excited. My wife was excited. The kids were especially excited because we were taking them to a huge waterpark. We were all set to go.

The day before we were to leave, I went in to see my podiatrist. I had an infection in my left foot, probably caused by some minor injury.

The podiatrist and I had been working on this for weeks. I'd seen him several times prior.

I had some uneasiness in the back of my mind, but things seemed to be going along with some success. So, we were planning to leave for our vacation the next day.

There was some increased bleeding and some dark spots on my foot, but I didn't see that as a showstopper. I was mentally planning how to get around that on our trip. I could rent a walker or use crutches. But it was our only vacation all summer and I wasn't about to ruin my family's trip over this. No way…not gonna happen!

What happened *next* was definitely one of those don't-blink-because-life-comes-at-you-quick moments.

When the podiatrist saw my left foot, he had a very worried look on his face. He called in another doctor. And together, they told me that the infection had gone into geometric replication, leading to sepsis. There was only one way that they infection could be stopped, and I didn't like it.

They looked at me, with a somber and serious look on their faces. The podiatrist told me plainly and seriously, "You could go on My trip, but you'd be dead by Sunday." Then they both looked at me and said, *"This infection cannot be stopped. You could either lose your leg, or you could lose your life. It's up to you."*

I had to make an unpleasant but clear decision. And it didn't take long to make. My science background was the "third opinion" and I knew that the procedure had to be done. I called my beloved wife, Jackie, and told her what was going on and what was coming.

Things went from serious to *surreal* very quickly.

I asked Jackie to go on the trip without me – don't ruin things on my account, you know. But before the words even left me, I knew that this was *not* an option. Of course, she refused.

Our son Michael overheard the word "amputation" and got genuinely concerned.

This is one of those times where you just know that your life, and the lives of those around you, has just been altered, probably permanently.

They admitted me to the hospital next door.

The next day at 1pm, the orthopedic surgeon with the general surgeon, were both scheduled to perform a below-the-knee (BKA) amputation on my left leg.

Before they put me under, I asked the surgeon if I could say something first, and then also pray over the procedure and for everyone there. He approved my request.

First, I thanked everyone there for their expertise, their knowledge, and for taking such good care of me. Then I prayed for each of them, that Father God would give them wisdom and peace and that all would go well. I could feel the presence of Jesus in that operating room.

They gave me the anesthetic…I went out in *seconds*.

Later that day I awoke from the anesthetic with part of my left leg *gone*.

So, I was up to bat and life threw me a curveball, a life-altering permanent challenge. And I swung with *all* I had…

The Day After

That day was kind of a blur. The anesthetic was still wearing off, they had me on pain meds, and I was just plain tired. Of course, nurses came in throughout the night to administer I.V.s, I.V.-based antibiotics, give me water and empty my portable urinal, and give me pills.

I was in the hospital for 4 nights, each night seemed longer than the night before.

Weathering My Hospital Stay

Hospitals can be noisy, busy places and sometimes not very favorable for sleeping. The nurses were all great and I didn't mind their many visits throughout the day and night.

Because of the COVID-19 crisis, even my wife couldn't visit me, so any company was appreciated.

But the one thing that did get to me was the I.V. pump.

The pump is there to make sure that the fluids and meds are delivered correctly. But it also made sounds. Sounds that eventually drove me near crazy.

If you've even been in a hospital room with one, you know exactly what I mean. The pump worked by rotating a nylon gear within a plastic housing. The gear has slots where valving happens. The valves are activated by a ball bearing that rotated in one of the slots in the nylon gear. The ball bearing would drop and bounce on every turn. It was the bouncing sound that got to me. That never-ending *"wurrr... deet......deet...deet.deet, wurrr deet......deet...deet.deet"*.

And they put a special sleeve on my right (good) leg to make sure that no clots formed. It was like a mini version of pressure suits worn by jet fighter pilots. It was fine at first, but after a few hours it started to sound like a tractor, and it kept waking me up. *"Grrrr... bluuuunnnnn... Grrrrrrr..."*

OK, enough venting.

Seriously, though, weathering my hospital stay was all about being **grateful**, **positive**, **hopeful**, and **forward thinking**.

I intentionally thanked each and every person who cared for me. I forced myself to smile (it *does* make a difference).

I would *not* allow a single *"what if, how come, if only"* thought, any real estate inside my head. I refused to think back on what had just happened or entertain thoughts of *"what if the podiatrist had done..."*.

Instead, I disciplined myself to think about *"What now? How do I make the most of this situation?"*

Practice Positivity

I remember laying on the hospital bed the day after the amputation and starting to think to myself, *"What do I do now? How do I live life now? What if (insert some negativity and fear)?"*

Almost immediately, a voice in my head, I believe it was inspired by God, said, *"I'm going to do what it takes to overcome this. I'll live life in a new light. I can do it. I got this!"*

That is positivity.

When we face the uncertainty of life, we throw our shoulders back and proclaim the best, the brightest. Think about it, since we don't **know** what will happen in the future, why not **assume** that good will happen rather than bad?

Studies have shown over and over that we subconsciously move our lives in the direction of our expectations. Every aspect of life that we can affect or control, we do so in the direction of our beliefs, or expectations. So why not expect the best? Right?

Now, I am *not* a natural-born optimist.

In fact, I used to take pride in my natural ability to find the worst-case scenario in pretty much every situation in life. I was *so* good at it that I saw the worst that could happen and began to expect it.

I was constantly waiting for the "other shoe to drop" (no pun intended).

And guess what? The worst, or at least worse than should have happened, did happen with regularity. So much for being a pessimist.

For any of my fellow natural-born worst-case scenario pessimists, let me just say this – STOP IT RIGHT NOW!

I know that the thought of becoming a dyed-in-the-wool optimist sounds like, well, a worst-case scenario, it's really not that bad at all. In fact, you'll get to love it after a while.

Start small, and work your way up. Practice being unstoppably positive for 5 minutes a day and work up from there.

Try to think and declare out loud the best when you encounter the next unknown situation. It doesn't cost a penny, and it doesn't hurt at all.

Then watch your life improve as you consistently apply positivity. It really *does* work.

Practice Gratitude

"What, practice gratitude?! I just lost a limb!"

Yes, that's true, but I'm still alive.

In my case, had I *not* had my amputation, I wouldn't be writing this book and you would not be reading it, because I would have died!

The thing with gratitude is that ***it's work***. It's effort. But like weight training, it strengthens you as you apply it.

Start off just saying, *"I'm thankful to be alive."* In my case, I still have my wonderful, healthy, strong right leg and I am thankful for it.

Also, my health is *so* much better than before the amputation and I am thankful for that.

Keep practicing gratitude and it will soon become automatic. Just a part of your life.

The biggest gain is that as we practice gratitude, we become happier and healthier persons. We are more enjoyable to be around. Life is just plain better and more enjoyable.

Evict "If Only…"

There is always a temptation to start saying to ourselves, *"If only I had done…"* or *"If only the doctor had known or done…"* DON'T GO THERE. EVER.

Not only will it not make anything better, but it will actually make things worse. *"If only…"* is the enemy of our souls. It will rob us of life, health, happiness, time, and opportunity if we let it.

The proper way to deal with "If only…" is to kick its scrawny, evil, bitter ass out of our mind, health, and soul!

Gratitude is the boot that we use to do this. It's a steel-toed boot with a pointy tip. Be thankful for what you have and "If only…" takes the bus out of Dodge every time.

OK, off the soap box… for now.

Phantom Sensations

Another tactic to keep things fresh, was to come up with new experiences and keep my mind active and engaged. My science background helped out in particular experiment…

One of the weirdest experiences that any amputee can have is *phantom sensations*. After removal of a limb, you still feel it there, sometimes for months. A range of sensations have been reported by amputees, pain, itching, even warm, soft sand.

This happens for two reasons: The first reason is that the nerves that used to report the sensations from your now- missing leg are still there, to some extent and they are now bored and need something to do. So they repeat the stuff they did before.

They're also somewhat traumatized by the whole operation and so they get back *at* you.

The second reason is that your brain has been registering and recording sensations coming from that now-missing leg, for a long time (as in my case), and your brain needs time to transition and adjust to part of your limb being gone.

Remember I was asleep when the surgery took place, so my mind has no recollection of it.

The mind is an amazing thing! It can morph and adapt to changes. It's called *neuroplasticity*.

The brain will create high-speed connections to do things faster and more efficiently if that action is practiced over and over. We call it "muscle memory", but it's really the brain re-wiring itself.

But these structural changes can take time and repetition. Sudden changes kinda' throw off the brain and it has to adjust. This is true for amputations.

Phantom sensations are partially a by-product of our brains trying to reconcile with the missing limb.

This makes sense, right? Especially if your brain was not consciously registering sensations during the surgery (we hope). And so after surgery, you (and your brain) wake up and "poof" your leg is gone. This is a bit of a startling transition for your brain, so it keeps playing back previously recorded sensations.

So, when I awakened after the amputation, and for weeks or months afterward, my mind tried to reconcile the fact that there used to be a limb, with all its associated sensations there, and now there isn't.

The interesting thing is that the mind continues to replay pre-recorded sensations that are appropriate for the position of the remaining limb.

For example, you know if you rest your heel on a hard surface for too long, it feels uncomfortable and so you need to shift your position, right?

Well, this felt-need to shift my position happens when my left leg is in the correct position for a period of time, even if there is no longer a heel to feel anything!

Likewise, when I get up to go to the bathroom and I put my leg down, I can "feel" the carpet with my now missing foot!

It is *very* strange indeed. And this formed the basis of my experiment...

The Floating Leg Experiment

Ok, this is where my background in science comes into play. I formed a hypothesis about which sensations that my mind picks to replay.

I proposed that it uses the *position* of the now amputated limb. It uses the *most recent, most impressive, most often experienced* sensations. Just kinda' makes sense, right?

So, to test my hypothesis I came up with an experiment – while I was still in the hospital!

I realized in the middle of the night, that because of the infection and the resulting wound, there was a position that I simply could not place my leg into. It would cause bleeding and was too painful. I hypothesized that It had been long enough that my mind would no longer have a record of that position and the associated sensations to draw from.

Now the question was, how would the phantom sensation mechanism in my brain handle having no records to replay? What sensations would it create for my missing foot?

While in the hospital bed, I repositioned myself in *that* position and I quickly had my answer. And it was so weird, I could not have possibly imagined it!

My brain had no record to replay, so it created the sensation of **my left leg floating in space over the hospital bed!** It literally felt like my left leg was floating back and forth. I could see that it was, in fact resting on the bed and not moving at all. I touched the leg. Nope no floating, no moving.

But my mind felt it *had to* come up with something, and that the "something" was nothing. Science can be fun (and weird) sometimes.

These are the sorts of things I do to keep myself entertained.

CHAPTER 2

DEALING WITH CHANGE

T he fact is that we are constantly dealing with change.

How well we deal with change is a big determiner of how happy we are and the overall quality of our life.

Change Is A Challenge

As an amputee, I had to just plain say goodbye to some things. I used to run quite a bit in college. I played soccer and volleyball. I had to say "see you later" to these things. That said, I hope to get back there someday soon.

But some things I had to say goodbye to, like the simple act of getting up in the middle of the night and walking to go to the bathroom. This simply is not an option for me anymore. I must use my walker, my iWalk, or don my prosthetic leg. By the time that happens, I am now awake. And it takes time to get back to sleep…occasionally, a long while afterward.

This might sound simple and you might be saying to yourself, *"What's the big deal?"* The big deal to me is that this is for the **rest of my life**.

And there are other things like that.

I must think ahead if I want to go up and down the stairs. I can't just jump up and answer the doorbell. If I want to make myself a sandwich, I have to plan ahead, put on a mobility device, carry one thing at a time, and so on…

These things add up and sometimes the shear monotony of all the extra steps I have to take just to walk across the room can be a challenge in and of itself.

With a leg amputation, one of the challenges especially in the beginning, is falling. It is a possibility.

I had to retrain my balance and how I apportion my weight over my legs from using a walker at first, to the iWalk 2.0 Hands-free Crutch [https://amzn.to/ 2LtGiyg], and then to my prosthetic leg.

Jim's iWalk 2.0 – a "God-send"

In fact, before I got my prosthetic leg, the iWalk [https://amzn.to/2LtGiyg] worked so well that once, I *forgot* that my lower left leg was amputated, and I tried to "stand on it" and I fell.

Then when I tried to get up, yep, did it again and fell again.

> *The key to falling is to make sure that you always get back up again.*

This simple statement is really a metaphor for life – I just make sure that I keep getting back up, regardless of how hard the fall.

Change Is an Opportunity

I used to dislike change, probably even feared it.

I saw change as the enemy, a foe seeking to destroy me. I saw change as things getting worse. This is because I used to be a pessimist, remember?

For a pessimist, any change is "going to be bad" and the best hope is to work to keep things as they are.

This might seem crazy to a non-pessimist, but it makes perfectly good sense to those of us who are craz…I mean pessimists.

But as I experienced life more, especially after getting married to the most beautiful and amazing woman in the world and having two amazing kids, I grew to see change for what it really is – an *opportunity*.

This makes so much sense now, right?

If we never change, we will always be the same, have the same things, do the same things, and experience the same things. Where's the fun in that? We were created to grow and change.

The last 15 years have brought me amazing things – I went from 350 pounds and on the express lane towards death to my ideal weight and in great health, getting married to the most amazing woman in the universe, having two wonderful kids together, getting my dream job as a software developer, and many other gifts!

When I think about the amazing changes, I thank God for *change*.

Take time for God

I don't know if you're a person of faith. I'm a follower of Jesus Christ.

On September 12, 1975 at 8:32 PM, I confessed my need for Jesus and began the most important relationship of my life. And like most, my life has been somewhat of a roller coaster.

There were good times, bad times, great times, sad times, and mad times. But through the whole thing, Jesus has always been there, right next to me in that roller coaster cart. He has never abandoned me, even in times when it seemed that pretty much everyone else did.

And through this whole journey of amputation and rehab, He's right there, cheering me on. He is my strength and joy.

If I've never considered Christ Jesus, please take some time to do so.

CHAPTER 3

WORKING THROUGH LOSS

Quite frankly, this chapter was the most difficult for me to write. To work through. In case you haven't picked it up, I'm a classic, hard-working, "deal-with-it-and move-on" type of guy. I'm not "touchy-feely" to say the least. I'm a "steady-as-you-go" man.

I once had a manager at work (Microsoft) tell me, *"Jim, if you were on fire, we wouldn't know except for the smoke."* That pretty much sums it up.

So, working through the emotional journey of loss that is part-and-parcel of having an amputation, was difficult for me. Difficult but necessary.

Fending Off the Imagined Losses

Loss can come in the form of the *fear* of loss or the *feeling* of loss. It's imaginary, but it sure feels real at the time. Any life change can involve this imaginary loss, especially a change like amputation.

In my case, the amputation was caused because of an unstoppable infection, so, naturally, I had the fear that it would crop up again. Dealing with this took a lot of faith, time with God, and telling myself over and over again, "Ain't gonna' happen!"

But it also took action. **Nothing destroys fear like action.**

I studied hard to make sure I knew everything I could about infections associated with amputations. I studied nutrition. I studied exercise. I studied treatments. I suffered through three weeks of antibiotics and all the "fun" associated with that. I did what my doctor told me to do. I did everything I could to avoid a re-infection.

But it also took a revelation from God.

During the gut rebuilding process, I had had enough of the process and was in the middle of a "just shoot me now" moment, when God spoke to me. It was in the middle of the night on a routine potty stop and I sat there asking Him, "How long, oh Lord?" I had hit a wall and it seemed like it was over for me.

God told me, "**Total Eradication**." He wanted any trace of infection, all those things that had polluted me to be eliminated once for all!

This gave me hope and I knew that He had a purpose in it all. In fact, knowing that God has a purpose for tough things always brings faith and hope.

Romans 8:28 (NKJV) says: "And we know that *all things* work together for good to those who love God, to those who are called according to His purpose." (emphasis mine)

All things, even an *amputation*. For *my* good.

One of the things that any major life change can produce is fear. And for men specifically, this is the fear that "I am no longer as much a man as I was." Or that I am now "half the man I used to be."

This is a real thing because a man's self-identity rests a lot on what he can do, how he provides for his family, what he can achieve.

An amputation can stoke the fires of this fear in a unique way because amputations limit mobility and a man's ability to perform.

The fear is that the limits are extensive and permanent and that those limits would reduce a man to *less than* a man.

Now, all of these things are false, as any irrational fear is, but they sure *feel* real in the muck of the moment. And my imagination could take advantage of that fear and attempt to solidify it in my mind.

So, my trick to defeating this fear, as is the case for all fear is **action**. I worked hard to increase my mobility, to strengthen myself, to take care of myself.

I also take the time to work through the emotions and all the thoughts that come with this fear.

The conversations went something like this:

Fear: *"You're just a burden to those who care about you the most."*

Me: Those who really care about me will never see helping me as a "burden." Besides, I'm back to nearly 100% mobility and function. My dear wife and our wonderful kids love helping me. We're all stronger now. That's not a burden, it's a benefit.

Fear: *"You won't be there for your kids like you were before."*

Me: Yes, I will. More in fact, because they see me working through this whole thing and that teaches them lessons on faith and resolve that they couldn't learn *any* other way. Seeing me work through the losses helps them to do the same with faith and wisdom in ways I can't even grasp.

Fear: *"Your wife sees you as less of a man and you don't make her happy anymore."*

Me: No, she doesn't see me as less but more because I'm handling this with faith and strength. And *that's* sexy. And yes, I do make her happy because being a man isn't' about having all my parts but having a heart. And my heart is stronger than it has ever been.

Fear: *"Your colleagues won't respect you as much."*

Me: Yes, they will – more in fact because they see me being real and strong during this whole thing and they know that I'm working even harder to be there for them.

Fear: *"What will it be like when you're older? How will you even function?"*

Me: Ask me that after I finish my triathlon, jackass.

Working Through the Real Losses

The fact is that loss always involves a real removal of resources, to do what we need to do or want to do.

These losses are real and sometimes permanent. This requires working through these losses emotionally, personally, and adjusting life in response to the losses.

This of course, sounds easy enough. But for some, me especially, working though these losses emotionally was, and still is, a challenge.

I would prefer to be pragmatic and deal with the adjusting phase and just skip over the emotional part altogether.

But this isn't reality, and the truth is we are *all* emotional beings whether we want to admit it or not.

Our emotions affect pretty much every area of our lives. If we do not work through loss emotionally, we will be stuck in the past and incapable of really making the adjustments we need to.

For me, the "tell" is my motivation to forge ahead. If I feel like staying in bed well beyond the time to get up and get going, then I'm *off* emotionally, and I need to deal with loss.

The one immediate and obvious real loss is the loss of *mobility*.

This loss comes in two varieties: loss of *impulse* mobility and loss of *absolute* mobility.

Impulse mobility is where I want to get up in the middle of the night and go to the bathroom or when the doorbell rings and I'm upstairs and I want to go down and answer the door. Before, I could just do these things without really having to think about them.

Now, of course, in order to go from no prosthetic to moving around takes longer and is more involved. Even simple things take longer.

That said, I am getting faster on donning my prosthetic leg, and getting faster at getting around. But there will always be a *larger* barrier in the way of impulsive mobility.

Every single time I want to just get up and do something, I am reminded of this fact. There is nothing I can do about it and it won't go away. It is real.

Then there is *absolute mobility* – the loss of what I can do *after* the amputation. This puts limits on me to some degree.

Even the best-fitting, most advanced prosthetic leg will not provide the level of total mobility that my real leg can offer. It comes *really* close though, but not 100%.

My prosthetic leg is amazing! It fits well and now that I'm proficient at using it, I prefer it over the iWalk [https://amzn.to/2LtGiyg]. It gives me almost 100% mobility. But it will never replace my leg. This is a real, tangible loss.

Some days I am OK with this and I just move on. Other days, it hits me harder and I have to process the emotions I am having. I **allow** myself to *feel* them. I identify them, I *acknowledge* them – that they are real, that they are appropriate, and they are important. ***But they don't determine my reality – they're just part of it***.

I am not a psychologist, nor do I play one on TV, but I know these things must happen for me to heal emotionally.

If I tried to just white-knuckle it and "get over it and move on", then I stifle healing, progress, and growth – behind my own stubbornness and resolve.

The loss is real, and it stinks.

Yet I am profoundly grateful for my prosthetic, the iWalk [https://amzn.to/2LtGiyg], my walker, and all the various things I have used, to help me move around. But I would trade them all and a life-time supply of really good chocolate to get my leg back.

Dealing with the emotions of this real loss in a healthy way, helps keep me whole and grounded in reality. It helps me stay on the field rather than slinking off to the bleachers.

But dealing with emotions is also about *reorienting* them. After all the acknowledging, accepting and coddling of my tender emotions, I can then be the Drill Sergeant again and tell my emotions to focus on another part of reality – the goodness of God in the midst of tremendous loss.

Regarding my conversations with the fears I shared with you above, there is a silver lining to the amputation cloud.

A gold lining in fact. Because for every real loss there are also real gains.

Working Through Sorrow

I am certainly no cry baby, but this whole experience has really brought me closer to my feelings, especially sorrow. And one of the things about sorrow is it can strike suddenly and at odd times.

For example, I lost my Dad about 20 years ago, my Mom about 10 years ago, and my older brother years ago. So, these occurred a while ago and I'm over them, right? Nope.

Even today, I'll be in a situation that will remind me of one of them, or that I might turn to them and say some inside joke, and they're not there. Then I'll get sad and the tears will come.

It's the same with my leg. I miss my leg.

Once when I was watching a YouTube video on what to expect after an amputation, I just started crying, sobbing uncontrollably as waves of sorrow and loss washed over me.

Every time the doorbell rings and there's no one else to get it for me, I feel sad.

The loss is real and tangible. I don't try to "buck up" anymore. I let it happen. And equally important, I *don't* put myself down for it. I accept it as part of the healing process, part of me.

But as I said earlier, though the loss is real, there are also real benefits as I intentionally work through the loss and work with my emotions, instead of trying to keep them quiet or squelch them, or sweep them under the rug. Focusing my emotions on these helps me to return to the new normal.

CHAPTER 4

RETURNING TO THE NEW NORMAL

T his all happened in the year 2020 – what will be called in the annals of history as the Stupidest Year in History.

It was a year of unprecedented change, few of them good. I call 2020 the "Beta version of 2021".

A lot of people told us we had to get used to the "new normal" – wearing masks even though these didn't help, shutting down schools and churches while bars and abortion clinics "had" to stay open, and the term "social distancing" was mandated, which I hope in the near future, I'll never have to hear – ever again.

The fact is that all of us are constantly adjusting to a new normal, right?

After we learn to walk, do we ever go back to crawling? When you graduate from a school, do you keep going back? When we get married, do we continue acting like we're single? (Hint – if you do this long enough, you will be single again.)

You get the point – we are always adjusting to a "new normal". But we also want and need some level of consistency and continuity in life.

So, my story is also about returning to normal, or as "normal" as I can make it. There are obviously some changes that will never go away, and certain challenges will always be before me, but with persistence, fearlessness, and hard work, I know that I can return to normal living. It's a new normal, a better normal.

Returning to "normal" for a BKA amputee, and for most amputees, is about steadily *increasing* mobility, strength, getting back to doing what you did before, and even going *beyond* that.

During this journey there are challenges, missteps, falls, disappointments, setbacks, and triumphs. Kinda' sounds like life doesn't it?

Going Home

Part of returning to the *new normal* was going home.

The very first day back from the hospital was pretty much a blur. But I *definitely* remember trying to get up the front steps of our home, and upstairs to my bed. I will remember this for a long while because it was a fond mixture of humiliation and the wonderful help of family.

I was used to carrying my own weight *all* my life and *wasn't* used to getting help! I was *stubbornly* independent. This *had* to change, and God knew exactly how to end it.

Coming home from the hospital, I was basically a big, weak blob and couldn't help much. I had to be dragged up the stairs by my brother-in-law – Tong, and my wonderful wife.

I tried with *all my might* to scoot up the stairs on my butt, but that didn't help much because I was still very weak from the surgery and being in bed the entire time at the hospital. So Tong and Jackie were stuck lifting almost all my weight using a gait belt around my upper body.

And when we got to my bed, even then they had to lift me from the floor into bed!

At present, I'm happy to say that I can now easily go up and down the stairs, get in and out of bed, get off the floor, drive our vehicles, and even walk around a track!

But I wasn't able to do *any* of that for a while – and the whole experience grated against my nature. Yet God was using this to reform my attitudes, teach me how to receive, and strengthen my practice of gratefulness.

During the weeks after July 10, 2020, I was increasing in strength, mobility, and the ability to take care of myself, but I still needed a lot of help. I couldn't go up and down the stairs. I had a walker but was still tentative on it.

Eventually I graduated from the walker to the iWalk [check it out here: https://amzn.to/2LtGiyg] *and* a cane.

Then three and a half months after surgery, I got my prosthetic. It was all a process and it required grit, persistence, and humility.

It still does.

I talk about mobility in some detail in the next chapter.

Home Care Nursing

One of the decisions that we made was to get some professional help.

My wife is awesome! She is an accomplished pianist and musician, her book publishing business is growing by leaps and bounds, and she's a world-class communicator. As I write this, she is also an eight-time #1 International Bestselling author. And she is awesomely beautiful to boot. It is an amazing *understatement* to say that I married up, *way* up!

But she ain't no nurse, nor do I want her to be.

Jackie has done an amazing job at many things, especially since she picked me up from the hospital.

But as a gift to her, I hired a home care nurse.

This was especially important in the first couple of weeks because I had wounds that needed dressing, and we both agreed that it was a good idea to track my vitals shortly after I had come home.

Turns out that this was a good idea, because my blood oxygen level was low, and the home nurse was able to suggest breathing exercises to get it back to where it needed to be for optimal healing.

The home nurse also trained both Jackie and me how to dress the wounds.

Home care nursing is not that expensive, and it's worth every penny.

Our insurance didn't cover home care nursing, and we ended up paying out-of-pocket, but I'd do it again.

A Word to Caregivers and Family

The journey that the amputee is on, is a challenging one, full of advances and retreats. Thank you for being there for them. Your presence and help mean more to them than they can say.

You have taken on a lot more work to support your loved one, work that could take a toll on you. So be sure to take time for yourself.

Remember that the journey is going somewhere – life as it should be.

A danger lies in your getting too used to your role as caregiver and wanting to, at some point, keep the amputee "safe."

You want to minimize falls, reach out, help, and serve the amputee.

While this is really needed in the beginning stages of this journey, as the amputee gains mobility and moves back to taking care of themselves, one of the hardest parts is to back-off and let them.

We need to follow the wisdom, *"Never do for someone what they can, and should, do for themselves."*

And sometimes it's difficult to back away and let the amputee do more and more. Not to mention that some things just take longer for the amputee to do.

But though it takes longer, letting the amputee do things for themselves is really what is best for them, *and* for you.

Resist the temptation to treat the amputee as a "cripple" and as someone who always needs your help.

Now, put the shoe on the other foot (pun intended) – do **not** allow the amputee to continually depend upon you. They should be progressing in their mobility and doing more for themselves as time goes by and it is part of your job as a caregiver or family member to make them do more.

Sometimes we need that. And we need your help to keep from treating ourselves as "cripples" too.

Remember this is a journey, not a destination, and the landscape should change as the amputee progresses. At first, they will need a lot of help, for almost everything.

As we gain more mobility, we need less help.

In the end, we should be back at full speed and doing pretty much everything we did before, if not more.

I remember the first day I was back from the hospital. I could barely do anything for myself. It was horrible!

Eventually, I was getting around better, especially when I got my iWalk [https://amzn.to/2LtGiyg]. I could then manage the stairs.

After several days, I even drove around our neighborhood! I remember how exhilarated I felt when I first drove our van, especially after weeks of being cooped up at home!

The day came when I finally got my prosthetic, and I could navigate the stairs pretty well. We, as a family, went places together – and I drove!

As I got trained on my prosthetic, my mobility improved by leaps and bounds such that I was able to eventually walk around well *without* a cane!

It is a process. And I am so thankful for those around me who helped, especially my beloved wife, Jackie.

And the journey went somewhere.

Today, I can do everything myself. I even let my wife get away for the weekend alone while I took care of our kiddos!

This process is important not only to the amputee, but for you the caregiver as well.

Remember: Amputation is a challenge *not* a life sentence. The amputation is permanent, but most of the challenges are *temporary*. And so is your job as a caregiver.

Eventually, you will step away from that role and get back to your previous role.

Don't get too attached to your caregiver role, and don't try to derive too much value from it – it's *temporary*. The more temporary, the better.

A Word to the Amputee

Amputee to amputee, let me say this -- amputation is a challenge *not* a sentence. The amputation is permanent, but most of the challenges are *temporary*.

Don't take on the identity of the reality – don't let yourself be labeled a "cripple" and don't take it on as a lifestyle.

Amputation is a speedbump in life, not the end of the road.

This is a *super* important TIP: Make *daily* mobility goals for yourself. Make progress every day.

They don't have to be big goals, but they have to be progress. You decide how *far* and how *fast*.

And don't stay stagnant...life is too precious to waste.

Be courageous and fearless. Strive to live better.

Develop a fighter's attitude. Get angry at complacency. Get motivated. Get going.

As you can tell from my conversations with *fear* earlier, I developed a 'tude. I became a fighter. I WILL win. I will *not* be beaten!

I subscribe to a periodical from the Amputee Coalition. In one issue there was an astonishing story about a guy who owned a tree service. He loved what he did.

One day he fell, and his leg got taken by the chipper. Yet within months he was back at it...climbing trees and doin' his thing *with a prosthetic!!*

Man, that is double-tough. His story really inspired me to go further, try harder, and to NEVER let myself be a "cripple".

The Lesson: Never accept anything but the best *for* yourself and never expect anything less than the best *from* yourself.

My personal goal is to do more *after* my amputation than before.

I was athletic in college and I slowed down as life went on. But I'm not going to accept that from myself. I will go *way beyond* what I was doing *before* the amputation.

I'm committed to becoming more mobile. I will get out and walk every day. I will play soccer again. I will do a 5K. And I'll train to do a mini-triathlon.

> "**The Lesson:** Never accept anything but the best *for* yourself and never expect anything less than the best *from* yourself."
>
> – *James Morey*

They say the best revenge is success.

The best "revenge" on your amputation is to go **beyond** where you were before and tell that amputation that it doesn't define you, limit you, or even slow you down!

The road back to normal isn't an easy one but it can be done, and you can do it!

May God be with you, Warrior!

CHAPTER 5

MOBILITY

A fter a leg amputation, regaining mobility is one of the *most important* goals an amputee can have.

A leg amputation is a mobility challenge, not an overall health challenge. There is a temptation to give in to a "crippled" mentality.

Constantly increasing my mobility helps keep me from this destructive mindset.

There is no reason that once I got trained on my prosthetic, that I couldn't have nearly 100% mobility. Even if I were a world-class sprinter before the amputation, I would've been set because they have sleek, cool carbon-fiber blades for that.

Mobility is also my key to becoming more *autonomous*. Increase my mobility and my world gets bigger. Increase my mobility and I increase my *confidence*.

I *refused* to get into the habit of having others do for me what I could do myself, even if it took longer and required more effort.

Yes, at first, I needed more help as I recovered from surgery and built my strength. But as I did, I added things every day that I did myself.

Most tasks were more difficult and took longer, but I strove to do all of those that I could by myself as soon as possible.

The Stages of Mobility

As part of regaining full mobility, I went through several phases with my amputation and prosthetic. The whole thing took from mid-July through the end of 2020, and is still in process.

This is my experience.

Note: Your mileage may vary, but this can also serve as a guide to help you form expectations and gain some familiarity with the process.

Stage 0 – The Amputation

The amputation happened on July 10, 2020. Not that the timing of any amputation is "good" but this one ruined our vacation plans and changed the course of the rest of my life. I spent 3 days in the hospital and went home on day 4.

Stage 1 – Recovery

The next month was basic recovery from the surgery. It started with almost zero mobility and ended in minor mobility.

My mobility really couldn't go anywhere until my surgery wounds had completely healed.

My main mobility device was my walker. Later on, I started to use the iWalk [https://amzn.to/2LtGiyg] to some degree.

Stage 2- Basic Mobility

Once my surgery wounds were well along in healing, I could get up and move around better. This is where I got my iWalk [https://amzn.to/2LtGiyg] and started to use it more and more. Near the end of this stage, I was able to go up and down the stairs.

Stage 3 – Getting My Prosthetic

By October, I had my check socket (a temporary socket for a loaner prosthetic) and was getting used to using the loaner prosthetic leg.

At first, I only used it for a little while and walked on the prosthetic leg with my walker.

After a week, no more walker, and I was using only a cane to assist me on the prosthetic.

Three weeks later, I had my final prosthetic and was getting around pretty good with a cane.

Within a week, I did not need a cane, except for outside where I used a 4-prong cane.

Stage 4 – Normal Mobility

By "normal" mobility I mean that I could go places by myself and pretty much take care of myself.

At this point, I didn't need much help at all, and in fact, was helping out others more and more. This felt awesome!

I was seeing both a physical therapist who specializes in amputation mobility, and also a personal trainer.

The PT specialist really knows her stuff and she has helped me retrain my gait and balance more than I thought possible.

The personal trainer, paid for by some very generous and caring friends, also has experience in helping amputees. He is pushing me along, and my recovery is blossoming because of him and the PT specialist.

At this stage I could do almost everything I could before, including dancing with my wife!

Stage 5 – Advanced Mobility

This is where I make good on my commitment to go beyond where I was before the amputation.

I cannot stress enough how important this is to winning!

My prosthetic specialist challenged me to enter and compete in a special triathlon for amputees in 2021 and gaining advanced mobility is part of that.

Advanced mobility is about playing soccer again, running again, swimming again, and in general, living life to the fullest regardless of the challenges of amputation.

As part of my new-found warrior attitude, I am gaining advanced mobility in order to vanquish any fear or limitation from the amputation.

Part of this is continuing to work with my PT specialist and also my personal trainer on advanced balance, flexibility, strength, and coordination.

This is not an easy road, but I am determined to complete that triathlon and more.

Building Up My Soul Strength

Amputations are both a mobility challenge and a mental challenge.

I needed to strengthen both my body *and* my soul.

The very nature of an amputation causes some isolation, especially early on, while regaining mobility. I couldn't get around so well in the early stages of rebuilding my mobility.

We used to take our kiddos to the local park together. For a while, anyway, I couldn't do that. I had to stay home.

During that time, especially the early stages, it was vital to take the time to strengthen my soul by engaging my family and community, by practicing positivity, by kicking out negative thoughts, especially any pesky "if only..." thoughts, and by taking time for God.

Engage My Family and Community

Here is the part where I get to brag on my **_amazing_**
wife, Jackie again. Let me reiterate that I married up
-- way up!

My Beloved has been a rock in this whole thing. She
has had to put up with so much – especially during
the gut rebuilding process – and has taken on a
huge burden of taking care of me. All of this
without a single complaint or a sharp word.

She's encouraged me, strengthened me, and has
kept me from getting far too mopey.

Aside from all of that, Jackie solely took care of our
rambunctious and imaginative nine-year-old
daughter and ten-and-a-half year old son, filling in
the gaps I left while I was regaining my mobility.

My Beloved deserves a medal or two!

Kindred Spirits

It was also important to remember, that I now
belong to *a very exclusive club*. A club so exclusive
that it literally costs an arm or leg to get in – the of
the community of amputees.

I reached out to an amputee community on Facebook and various other ways. I not only got vital information, but it helped to know that there are others out there that I can reach out to when I need to talk.

There are a number of helpful YouTube channels that can help not only in choosing the correct mobility device, but also just knowing that there are others out there who understand has been encouraging.

I'll list some of my favorite resources later in this book.

There are also support groups both locally and online.

Building Up My Physical Strength

One of the most important factors in my continued mobility is building up my arm, leg, and abs strength. Just using a walker did this to some degree, but I also did daily exercises to build strength as I increased my mobility.

Physical Therapy

A physical therapist dropped by my hospital room and assessed my post-operative mobility. She also gave me a sheet of paper with some PT exercises.

Physical Therapy has two important effects: 1) strengthen the leg that received the amputation and associated hip and ab muscles that would be important as I increased my mobility; 2) gets me involved in *my own care*.

This last point should not be overlooked. There is a huge and very real temptation, after an amputation, to give up or to give in to a "cripple" mindset.

The fact is that with today's medical and prosthetic technology, my road to absolute mobility was short, *unless* I didn't take my PT seriously. I also had to re-strengthen my leg, hip, and ab muscles.

Weight Training

The fact is, even after I was fitted and trained on my prosthetic leg, I'll still needed increased leg strength in my sound leg and in my upper body and arms. It's simply required for my mobility. Lifting weights really helped.

Avoiding Contracture

Contracture is where the muscles and tendons in the upper leg *contract*, because the leg is not used for regular mobility. Contracture usually sets in early in the healing and remobilizing process.

To help avoid contracture the hospital fit me with a "leg straightener", basically a knee brace, to keep the residual limb knee straight.

I had to wear it all day *every day* for a few weeks, and I grew to hate it. Yet it did a great job of helping me to avoid contracture.

Now, of course, with my prosthetic, I don't need to worry about contracture so much, although I still regularly stretch the quads and tendons.

Mobility Devices

This is a brief guide of the various mobility devices that an amputee might use. I hope you profit from this information.

NOTE – Wheelchairs, walkers and crutches will work for both above the knee (AKA) and below the knee (BKA) amputations. The iWalk [https://amzn.to/ 2LtGiyg] and Knee Scooter only work for BKAs.

Wheelchairs (AKA and BKA)

Suitable Uses: Flat surfaces or ramps; no stairs or rough or bumpy surfaces.

The ultimate in easy is a wheelchair, and you'll probably use these when visiting your doctor in the early stages.

Of course, a wheelchair is useless if you have stairs to navigate, but they are easy to get into and out of, and work very well on flat surfaces or ramps.

However, don't get too used to a wheelchair if you've had a single leg amputation. Do your best to move onto another mobility device as soon as practical because using a wheelchair for too long can cause muscle atrophy in the legs, hips, and abdomen.

It can also produce bad habits.

Walkers (AKA and BKA)

Suitable Uses: Flat surfaces or ramps; no stairs or rough or bumpy surfaces.

Your first mobility device will be a walker. Your walker is your friend and as you regularly use it, you'll get faster.

An added bonus is that your upper body and arms will get stronger. For those of you who are already buff, this isn't a big deal. For me it was.

However, it is nearly impossible, and certainly not safe, to go up and down stairs in a walker. And walkers are pretty useless on uneven or bumpy surfaces.

One thing to look out for in using a walker is to stay within the "balance zone" of the walker. That is, don't lean too far forward on the walker nor too far behind. You'll quickly discover the "balance zone" early on when using your walker.

One of the most useful things to get is a good carrying bag to attach to the walker. This allowed

me to carry stuff around. My beloved wife got me one that's very handy.

Check it out here: https://amzn.to/3noA MKp

One of its cool features is that it is fitted on the side of your walker, so it doesn't obstruct the pathway-view in front of you. You can see your foot/feet while walking, and lessen the possibility of tripping.

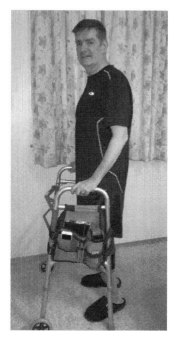

Jim on his prosthetic leg demonstrating where the carrying bag attaches to the walker.

One of the issues with walkers is that they tend to put too much pressure on wrists which could lead to wrist problems. But with practice, you'll learn how to use it properly. And when you use your walker as sparingly as possible, that will greatly reduce any potential wrist issues.

Crutches (AKA and BKA)

Suitable Uses: Flat surfaces or ramps; no stairs or rough or bumpy surfaces.

I didn't use crutches at all after my amputation. I just didn't feel balanced and safe. Some people really prefer crutches over walkers, so it's a personal choice.

Just like wheelchairs and walkers, crutches are of little use in going up and down stairs, and aren't suitable for uneven or bumpy surfaces.

One of the problems with crutches is that they tend to put too much pressure on wrists which could lead to wrist problems.

Knee Scooter (BKA Only)

Suitable Uses: Flat surfaces or ramps; no stairs or rough or bumpy surfaces.

I think that knee scooters are better than both walkers and crutches. I could rest part of my weight on the knee of the amputated leg (BKA only) and take that weight off my good leg. Because of this, it put less pressure on my wrists and doesn't cause wrist problems.

Like wheelchairs, walkers, and crutches, knee scooters are worthless in going up and down stairs and aren't suitable for uneven or bumpy surfaces. Also, I have heard folks who have used one, tell me that if I turned too quickly, I could tip over and fall.

Like the walker, I could get a carry bag and other accessories to "pimp my ride".

The iWalk2.0 (BKA Only)

NOTE – *Before I go on this seemingly over-exuberant rave about the iWalk, I want you to know that I have not received any compensation from iWalkFree, the company that manufactures the iWalk, nor any other party associated with them. I just really like the iWalk* [https://amzn.to/2LtGiyg].

Suitable Uses: Flat, uneven, or bumpy surfaces or ramps and stairs; pretty much anywhere I want to go, except ladders.

I was watching a YouTube video by another leg amputee and she started talking about the iWalk 2.0 Hands-Free crutch. I searched on the Interwebs and found the company's web page. And I'm truly glad I did.

The iWalk is intuitive to use, easy to learn, and remarkably restored my mobility to 80% plus. My bedroom is upstairs, and before the iWalk [https://amzn.to/2LtGiyg], getting up and down those stairs was a bear. It got easier as I got stronger, but it wasn't anywhere near 80%.

Within 15 minutes of learning the iWalk, I was strolling well and getting up and down the stairs was now possible without getting on my buttocks. Voila!

On top of this wonderful level of mobility, the iWalk also provides the following advantages over other mobility devices:

Keeps My Amputated Leg Strong

When scooting around on a walker or crutches, my amputated leg *doesn't* get any exercise.

If my amputated leg doesn't get exercise, the muscles in the upper leg, hips, and abs start to atrophy. This means when the time comes to train on my prosthetic, I'll also need to re-strengthen those muscles.

With the iWalk, *both* legs get exercised. The muscles in the upper leg, hips, and abs get exercised equivalent to walking. The iWalk is like an additional set of PT exercises every day.

Keeps My Balance in Tune

The movements with the iWalk take advantage of the balance and movements I had developed over my entire life. This is one reason it's so easy to learn.

It also helps to keep balance in tune. This comes in very handy when the time comes to train on your prosthetic.

Keeps My Good Foot Safe

One of the disadvantages of a walker or crutches is that they force me to hop on my good foot. This might not be bad for a short while, but long-term this can put harmful stress on the good foot, ankle, and knee.

Over time this can negatively affect that sound leg.

Another thing to look for is *tilting* my good foot while standing. Remember, my *feet* were meant to distribute my weight over the entire area under the foot.

Now that I have only one foot, it puts twice the strain on my foot even with my foot placed flat.

And then if I tilt my foot, the edge of my foot now must bear the entire weight, which it was *not* designed to do.

If I stand and lean up against a wall, I'll tend to tilt the good foot in the direction of the wall, typically the wall on the good foot side. This can lead to problems with that foot. In my case this caused a sore to develop on the outside of my right foot.

I had to consciously plant my foot solidly when standing and leaning. I also used a lambs-wool slipper for padding.

With the iWalk, I was standing up straight and not leaning. This saved that good foot from the stress…hooray!

Helps Prepare Me for my Prosthesis

If I went too long without exercising or using my amputated leg, the muscles would've atrophied, and I would have begun to lose balance.

Using the iWalk kept this from happening. But it also trained me to use my prosthetic, because the walking motions are nearly identical to using a prosthetic!

This made training on my prosthetic easier and shorter.

Sometimes amputees are anxious about walking on a prosthetic leg. "Can I make it work? How will it feel?"

Well, the iWalk helps them to prepare for the prosthetic by giving them confidence in balancing and by getting them used to walking on an artificial object rather than their own leg.

Provides Extended Mobility

Of course, increased mobility is the core feature of the iWalk. Going up and down stairs with a walker is nearly impossible. Walking longer distances on crutches, a walker, or even a knee scooter is tiring and awkward.

With the iWalk, I could go walking, and even hiking! It performs well on uneven and bumpy surfaces – which would be impossible or very tricky with crutches, knee strollers, and walkers.

Hands Free

And now the best for last – with the iWalk, I have my hands free! No more holding things in my teeth. No more asking someone else to carry things for me. Using the iWalk [https://amzn.to/2LtGiyg] is as close to using my own prosthetic leg as possible.

For BKA Amputees?

One important note is that the iWalk website explicitly says that BKA amputees can use the iWalk (https://iwalk-free.com/below-knee-amputation/). The page has a few good videos and some content about dealing with an amputation. Some amputees even bought and modified an iWalk for use in the shower! Imagine, showering standing up. This page is a great resource.

One modification is to remove the excess knee platform. It makes the iWalk more comfortable and lighter. The page also has instructions of how to do this properly.

The one requirement is that the residual limb below the knee must be at least four inches, which is typical for a BKA. Of course, speak with your doctor about using the iWalk before purchasing one.

Many, if not all of the sites and YouTube videos I saw of BKA amputees used it and found it extremely helpful, or was "a God-send" as one amputee called it.

I use a modified slipper (for my left foot) made of lamb's wool on the kneeling pad to make it more comfortable and to make it fit my tiny knee cap.

Falling and Getting Back Up

In a sense, regaining mobility after an amputation is like learning to walk all over again. And like the first time, falls happen.

It's just a part of the process and like we saw before the philosophy for falling is to keep getting up.

Your PT specialist will help you re-develop balance and that will reduce falling and might even eliminate it. Also, practicing with your mobility device definitely helps.

Falling and getting back up are a small reflection of the larger journey of dealing with an amputation, and really, life itself.

Life just plain is filled with challenges and sometimes we cruise through and sometimes we fall.

The trick is to just get back up, learn from it, and move on.

I fell, more than once. And the danger is not falling itself. *The danger is fear*.

If, after a fall, I fear falling again and back off from life because of it, then I lose.

One of my falls was while trying to throw something away. We have a foot-operate trash bin. I was using my iWalk and lifted the iWalk to step on the foot pedal to open the can. I got off balance a bit and reached out with my elbow (both hands were full) to lean against the wall. I missed the wall and fell backwards and on my left side.

OK, no big deal. I took off the iWalk and prepared to get back up. My wife, Jackie, brought over a chair to help me. I grabbed the chair and started to get up. That's when things went wrong.

I forgot I had taken off my iWalk and tried to put weight on my left foot (which isn't there anymore) and fell again.

This time I hit my left ribs on the corner of the chair on the way down and hurt them. It took about two weeks for the soreness in my ribs to heal.

That wasn't the real problem, though. The problem was that I was fearful of throwing anything away using our trash bin. And I didn't for a while.

Eventually, I *made myself* throw something away using that same trash bin. This time, no problems.

I overcame yet another obstacle!!

Protecting My Good Foot, Ankle, and Knee

Even with the best mobility device, my other foot and knee *still* sustain additional stresses when I move about.

You see, feet were designed by God to sustain *a lot of stress* as we humans walk, trot, run, and jump.

Yet continually putting too much of the *wrong* kind of stress on your foot isn't sustainable. And some of the stresses associated with amputations can put these stresses on your *good* foot.

Hopping, unaided by a mobility device, is the *worst!* It places a lot of stress on your good leg, hip, knee, ankle, and foot. Hopping around with the assistance of a walker is better.

But even with a well-fit prosthetic, your good foot, knee, and ankle has to put up with the abuse of daily mobility. So, you need to plan for that and take care of that foot.

Proper Footwear

Proper footwear is important even without an amputation. But with the added stresses associated with an amputation, well-fitting, and properly supporting footwear is essential. Not just any shoe will do.

I picked a good, sturdy sports shoe that is comfortable, and supports my arch, toes and heel well. Most of the name brands will do well here.

Some of the prosthetic manufacturers and associated companies have their own lines of everything from causal sports, and even formal wear. I haven't tried these yet, but I might when the time comes for new shoes.

Avoiding Strain

As I go about, I have to plan ahead and be a little more careful with every step. Avoiding abnormal strain on the good hip, knee, ankle, and foot are important to avoid injury.

Twisting tends to increase with walker use as I pivot round.

Using Leverage

One of the areas where strain can occur is in lifting myself up from a chair or bed to a standing position. This can put added stress on my arms and shoulders as well as the good knee.

One way to avoid excess strain is to use leverage. I make sure I'm not trying to stand from a position that is too low. This can put added strain on the good knee.

For example, my bed is kinda low, so I use a chair beside the bed as an intermediate platform. I certainly can go directly from the bed to my walker or whatever, but doing this several times a day can, over time, increase the chances of knee problems.

Prosthetic Leg

The ultimate mobility device is, of course, a good prosthetic leg. Prosthetic technology has reached amazing heights. There are prosthetics that work and look just like my real leg. There is a wide range of prices, styles, and capabilities to choose from.

NOTE – my actual prosthetic is shown below, and on the cover of this book. Pretty cool, isn't it?

The Device and Associated Stuff

Although the prosthetic is technically a mobility device, I put it here in its own section, because it's just *that* good.

As you already know, I am a big fan of the iWalk, but a properly-fitted prosthetic leg is far better.

The device (prosthetic) consists of three main parts: the socket (where my residual limb goes), the post (basically an aluminum tube with a fitting at the top that attaches to the socket and another fitting at the bottom that attaches to the ankle), and the foot (which is an ankle and a flat blade with an artificial molded foot around it).

I put a silicon sleeve around my residual limb that helps to cushion the limb and to create the vacuum that keeps the device on the limb.

On top of the sleeve, I might put a "sock" or two. Socks are specific-thickness cloth socks that are used to maintain the vacuum fit and comfort while using the device.

I typically start off the day with no socks and at noon add a #1 sock and again in the evening to maintain comfort and vacuum.

Another important accessory is the "shrinker" sock. This is like the adjustment socks, but is meant to apply gentle and constant pressure on the residual limb to keep it from swelling and to ensure that the limb fits into the socket.

My specialist started me off with a #5 shrinker and after my limb shrank enough, moved me to a #3 and then a #2, which I use today.

The shrinker is very comfy and helps to minimize *phantom pain*. [Remember the floating leg experiment?]

Mobility Ratings

With the wide variety of prosthetics available, it can be somewhat overwhelming to choose the right one.

Fortunately, my prosthetic specialist was key in helping me find the right combination of components.

The largest factor in choosing a BKA prosthetic is the mobility range, i.e. the rating of the ankle. These range from 1 [solid with no pivots, therefore, very little flexibility] to 4 with sports-like flexibility.

The ankle determines the mobility of the device. Some ankles are rigid, others are adjustable, and still others are carbon fiber blades used for athletics.

For most BKA amputees they will get a 2 to 3 mobility-range, multi-pivot, hydraulically dampened ankle.

Sounds cool, right?

This means that the ankle flexibility can be *easily* adjusted from moderate to excellent mobility as the amputee gets more adjusted to the prosthetic.

With my *sleek* prosthetic leg, I can adjust the range of motion and "looseness" of the ankle with two

Allen screws: one to control how the foot tilts up, and the other how the foot tilts down.

The post and sockets are pretty much standard parts, with the socket being custom-fit.

Fit and Tuning

Another especially important factor in using my prosthetic leg was the **fit** of the socket that accepts the residual limb *and* the **tuning** of the post angle and ankle adjustments.

The socket is specifically designed for comfort and support while using the prosthetic. It was molded from a scan of my residual limb and knee and is amazingly comfortable.

Typically, the prosthetic specialist will use a check socket – made of a heat-flexible plastic, to get the fit just right.

This could take a few visits with the specialist over a few weeks because the residual limb is dynamic and typically swells and shrinks over that period of time, even from hour to hour.

The purpose of the fitting period is to make sure that the permanent socket will fit within a reasonable tolerance. I call this the "sock range".

Socks are specific-thickness cloth socks that go over the prosthetic's sleeve that I can use to adjust the fit of my prosthetic.

The residual limb tends to be the largest in the morning and shrinks throughout the day as I wear my prosthetic. This is because use and wearing the prosthetic, forces fluids out of the residual limb throughout the day.

Ideally, I should fit snugly in my prosthetic with no socks in the morning and at night have on one or two #1 socks. When this happened and I had a comfortable fit, the prosthetic specialist ordered the permanent socket.

The permanent socket is typically made of carbon fiber and will last for 6 months to a year.

Eventually, my residual limb size became more stable and now I use a #1 sock throughout the day.

Tuning sessions are when the specialist had me walk back and forth to observe my gait. The specialist can tweak the adjustment-screws at the top of the post, *and* where the post attaches to the ankle.

These adjustments control the angle of the post, the angle that the foot has to the leg, *and* the outward adjustment of the post.

The adjustment fitting at the top of the post is an inverted pyramid with four screws on the four sides. To adjust the post angle, the specialist loosens the opposing screw and then tightens the opposite screw. He did this several times as I walked back and forth, until we had the angle *exactly right* in that single visit.

The adjustment fitting at the bottom, adjusts the angle of the foot inward or outward. The specialist adjusted my artificial foot to mirror my real (right) foot so that my gait and balance would be correct.

Getting these adjustments exactly right is important for getting your gait right. Fair warning: it might take a few visits to get it *just* right.

When everything is dialed in, you'll know it and your gait will be natural and steady.

Donning and Doffing

One of the important rituals with a prosthetic is putting it on – donning…and taking it off – doffing.

This has to be done several times a day to allow the residual limb to get some fresh air, to inspect it, to change socks, and to clean the sleeve.

Around the prosthetic is a flexible neoprene sleeve that rolls down when doffing, and is rolled up to seal the socket to the upper leg so that the vacuum is maintained. The vacuum keeps the prosthetic on.

To doff the device, I first rolled the outer sleeve down and then pulled my residual limb out of the device.

To don it, I insert my residual limb into the device then stand so that the limb can get pushed into the socket correctly with the assistance of gravity. Then I roll up the outer sleeve to maintain the vacuum.

Also important is to remember to put on my shrinker overnight.

One evening, I forgot to do this and the next morning, I couldn't get my residual limb into the socket of my prosthetic. It was frustrating! I had to wear the shrinker overnight to get it to fit again.

If the limb goes in too easily, I add a sock to maintain the correct fit.

Important note: If you forget to wear the shrinker overnight, your limb will likely get too big, to comfortably fit into the socket.

Caring for Your Residual Limb

Another daily task is taking care of your residual limb. This means keeping it clean, free from skin irritations, cuts, and infections.

I wash my residual limb with an all-natural *antifungal* soap. I use antifungal soap because the sleeve can cause sweating and in the warm, moist, and dark of the sleeve, fungus can grow.

Here's our affiliate link in case you'd like to check it out:

Rachelle Parker – Natural Handmade Essential Oil Artisan Soap Bars. Hypoallergenic, Anti-fungal Moisturizing Shea Butter, Coconut Oil & Jojoba Oil - Body Soap, Face Soap, Bath Soap Bars. Handmade Soap for Women & Men!

https://amzn.to/2LbQyeq

When I first started to wear the sleeve, I got a red rash on my upper leg and had to go without the prosthesis for a few days to let it heal.

At present, with regular washing of both the sleeve and my residual limb, things are good now.

I also inspect my residual limb nightly to make sure it's free from rashes, cuts, infections, or any other signs of trouble.

Prosthetic-Friendly Clothing

Wearing a prosthetic can cause some clothing challenges, especially pants.

The prosthetic is thicker than your leg, and getting pants that fit right can be challenging.

When you add the need to change the sock to adjust for fit on the prosthetic, and the additional need to go to the bathroom to do this privately, the challenge requires a solution!

In my case, we found the solution via a YouTube video – and all it required was a pant leg alteration.

My wife asked her friend who does alterations, to help us with this project.

We dropped off three pairs of my existing pants at this friend's home – two pairs of jeans and a pair of my best blue business suit pants.

She expertly sewed a zipper up each of the inner inseams on the left pant leg of these three pairs of pants, from the bottom to about 6 inches past the knee.

They were indeed *long* zippers.

Wow, what a breeze! Now I can simply unzip the zipper, change my sock, zip it back down, without having to go to the restroom...and no one knows any different.

This solved both problems at once!

I also wear oversized sweatpants, only in the house.

CHAPTER 6
ANTIBIOTICS

Antibiotics are medicines that help us fight infection caused by harmful bacteria and/or fungi.

Some of the antibiotics are targeted to a specific set of harmful bacteria. Most, however, are called "wide spectrum" antibiotics, which kill a wide variety of bad "bugs".

The problem is that antibiotics, especially oral antibiotics, can cause digestive problems, especially *diarrhea*.

This requires a Gut Rebuilding Program (GRP) as I call it.

In this chapter I'll discuss my experiences and share what I have learned with everyone who needs to take oral antibiotics, especially several rounds of these.

IV Antibiotics

While I was in the hospital, they gave me antibiotics intravenously (IV). These antibiotics go directly into my blood stream and do not pass through my digestive system, so the effects on my digestive processes were minimal.

Oral Antibiotics

If you have to take oral antibiotics for longer than just a few days, you may grow to hate them.

Yes, they will save your life, but they will also cause digestive problems, namely, diarrhea.

And I don't mean the **polite type of diarrhea** that calmly taps you on the shoulder and says, "*So, you might want to wrap up this conversation and head to the bathroom. No rush. Just FYI.*"

No. We're talking about **rude diarrhea**, the kind that doesn't tap you on the shoulder, doesn't give you any warning whatsoever!

It just whispers maniacally in your ear, usually *after* the fact, "*Bombs away, dude.*"

The reason is that oral antibiotics must pass through the digestive track to be absorbed, get into the blood stream, and do their job.

The problem is that these antibiotics use a "scorched earth" method. They don't just kill a specific range of bacteria; instead, they use pharmaceutical napalm and kill *everything* in their path – both the bad bacteria, and the good bacteria!

This causes the food we eat to flow through our guts at *near* light speed.

Literally, after a week or two of oral antibiotics, I would eat something and a few minutes later, I had better head to the can… or else.

This was my experience, and it prompted me… no this **required** me to come up with a solution.

The ironic thing is that after laying waste to my digestive track and minimizing my ability to absorb things, these oral antibiotics lower their own absorption rate – thus, *becoming less* effective! Go figure.

Maintaining My Gut Health

I learned the hard way that maintaining the health of my intestines and colon during the oral antibiotic regime is far better than letting it get devastated by the oral antibiotics and then having to rebuild.

One of the best strategies to maintain intestine health while also taking oral antibiotics, is to never let our guts be devastated by the oral antibiotics in the first place.

Get a bottle of good *probiotics* and take one – 2 hours after the oral antibiotics. This will rebuild the guts while they are still reasonably healthy. Let's talk more about probiotics later in this chapter.

Rebuilding My Gut

So, what do I do after I've taken my last oral antibiotic?

I need to rebuild my gut, even if I've been diligent about taking probiotics along with the oral antibiotics.

The extent of the damage to my gut, and the effort and time to rebuild my gut will vary with the type of oral antibiotics, the length I've taken them, and other factors.

In my experience, I was on oral antibiotics for *three* weeks, I didn't take any probiotics along with the oral antibiotics (not smart), and it took about *five long weeks* to rebuild my gut using the probiotics listed below.

Your experience might be longer, if you're taking *multiple* antibiotics, or taking them over a *prolonged* period of time.

Rebuilding the gut involves three basic parts: 1) rebuilding the mucus lining of the intestines (that are home to "good guy" bacteria ad fungus); 2) reducing or eliminating "bad guy" bacteria and fungus; and 3) repopulating "good guy" bacteria and fungus – also called "*probiotics*".

Probiotics

Our intestines are home to billions of bacteria and yeasts. Some of them are friendly and supposed to be there, and, in fact, necessary.

Some of them are neutral and don't affect anything.

Others of them are bad actors and can wreak havoc to our digestive system and our health in general.

The "good bugs" assist us in digesting and absorbing nutrients in our intestines. They are our friends. When I have too few of the good bugs or too many of the bad bugs, digestive problems, like diarrhea can result.

"Probiotics" is a label for all the good bugs.

Below are some examples and some foods rich in *probiotics*. Consuming these will go a long way toward rebuilding your gut.

Candidly, long after my several-week bout with diarrhea, I still take these probiotics periodically to keep my gut healthy. Everyone should be.

Probiotics are measured in CFUs, or Colony Forming Units.

Each CFU (good bug) can form an entire colony of other good bugs. The idea is that each of the good bugs will set up shop in our guts and raise a big happy family and help us to keep our digestive track from becoming a potato gun.

S. boulardii

Saccharomyces boulardii is a good-guy yeast that is resistant to stomach acid. It can make its way into our intestines, where it performs population control on bad bugs. This leaves more room for good bugs.

I found *S. boulardii* an indispensable friend while I was rebuilding my gut.

Life Extension Probiotics

The Life Extensions company provides quality health products.

I used their "Florassist GI with Phage Technology" probiotics capsules. These capsules contain many different species of probiotics and are double-chamber capsules that help the probiotics get as far into your intestines and colon as possible.

I call them *"Mission Impossible tracker pills"* because they look like something Ethan Hunt would swallow so that Luther or Benji could track him.

Fermented Foods

Fermented foods contain a boat load of probiotics. But you need to make sure that the foods are *not* cooked, because cooking will kill *most* if not all the helpful probiotics.

Typically, organic, fresh fermented foods are best.

Also, the fermented foods must be refrigerated. My favorites are listed below, but do your own research on Google, StartPage, Bing, Ecosia or GiveWater search engines and these will give you even *more* options.

Kefir

Kefir is a fermented dairy product that is absolutely packed with probiotics. Kefir comes plain or dressed up with fruit and some sugar for taste.

If you can handle the *plain* kefir with very little sugar, then that is best – because sugar feeds the bad bugs, especially **Candida albicans**, the worst of them.

Kefir can be cow-milk based or goat-milk based.

Goat milk is better – though more expensive and harder to find – because cow milk can be irritating to the gut.

Typically, kefir has 17 (or more) of the good bugs in billions of CFUs (Culture Forming Units).

If you're sensitive to milk, goat kefir is available through Whole Foods and other outlets.

Kimchi

Kimchi is a traditional Korean side dish that is basically spicy, fermented cabbage – naturally loaded with probiotics.

It comes in various levels of quality and spiciness. I happen to love kimchi, but you might not.

'Kraut

Sauerkraut is basically the German version of kimchi, without the spiciness. It is also packed with probiotics and it's much better on hotdogs than kimchi.

Foods That Help Defeat Diarrhea

In addition to our friends – the probiotics, there are foods that can also help you and me to show diarrhea the door.

These foods basically slow down digestion – and when one has diarrhea, slower is better.

The BRAT Diet

Another weapon in my anti-diarrhea arsenal is the BRAT diet. **BRAT** stands for **B**ananas, **R**ice, **A**pple Sauce and **T**oast. These things, according to lore, help to slow things down in the gut and let things solidify.

Bananas are especially good because they have soluble fiber and feed the good bugs in the gut. And they're rich in in potassium and other good minerals.

Protein

Solid proteins, such as steak, can also help things slow down, and slower is better when it comes to resolving diarrhea. This is because meat proteins, especially beef, are fibrous and protein takes longer to digest.

And because... steak.

Collagen Protein

We all need a good dose of protein, and protein helps slow down digestion (important during the Gut Rebuilding Program).

Especially helpful in gut rebuilding is collagen protein. It helps to stop "leaky gut" and to rebuild the mucus lining in the intestines.

I enjoyed shakes with collagen protein, kefir, water, and greens mix. The greens and collagen protein powder that we personally use can be purchased from https://store.drlivingood.com/.

Gelatin

Yes, gelatin. Gelatin is made from protein and it helps the intestines rebuild its critical mucus layer.

This mucus layer is where the good bugs live and do their thing for us.

Without the mucus layer, the good bugs have nowhere to settle down, raise a family, and build a community

You can use gelatin powder or eat sugar-free gelatin desserts. Be sure to use *sugar-free* gelatin (you'll find out why in a moment).

I used both, mixing the gelatin powder into my collagen protein shakes, as well as savoring sugar-free Jello dessert cups.

Here's the link to the unflavored gelatin powder we serendipitously found in our pantry and used for my smoothies:

https://amzn.to/396fRXj

Foods to Avoid While Rebuilding the Gut

Certain foods will slow down the gut recovery and might induce diarrhea. And we don't want that, do we?

Avoid Sugar and Starch

OK, I know that I just told you to eat bananas, rice, apple sauce, and toast to help solidify things down South.

However, there is a fine balancing act here.

The problem is that sugar (and starch, which my body quickly converts into sugar) also feeds the bad bugs in the gut. And the BRAT diet is pretty much *all* sugar and starch.

I know, *not* fair.

So, you'll have to experiment with how much and when to use the BRAT diet. In my experience I used the BRAT diet early in the Gut Rebuilding Project and ended as soon as things down there started to firm up.

I also used BRAT sparingly.

Things were going well, and I was getting some real BM goin' on and then I ate a gyro with the pita.

The next day I was back to food going through me like a freight train! Lesson learned.

Once I was all back to normal, then I resumed a normal diet, but I avoided sugars and starches for a while.

Avoid Vegetables

Yes, I know, pretty much every health expert says to eat more servings of veggies.

However, while rebuilding the gut, especially while still in the "Rude Diarrhea" stage, avoid eating vegetables, especially green leafy vegetables. That's because veggies help us to have smoother bowel movements.

When rebuilding our guts, smooth BMs aren't the problem. They will only exacerbate an already frustrating problem.

Depends

OK, I just had to get over myself and my fragile ego on this one. I was suffering from rude diarrhea and needed to get myself some Depends (or any adult "diaper") and wear them until I completely rebuilt my gut.

This saved me and my wonderful wife a lot of grief.

And I was sure to wait until I had three successful days of normal bowel movements before I stopped using them.

The first day was a false positive. Another lesson learned.

CHAPTER 7

PAIN MEDS

Codeine-based pain killers are amazing. But they are also very addictive. They can bring amazing relief and then turn around and destroy us without batting an eye.

Years ago, I had kidney stones. OMG, that was the worst pain I had ever felt!

I'd been cut, scraped, bruised, and broken more than my fair share during my life, but nothing could have prepared me for *that* level of pain – kidney stones...aargh!

It was a gnawing, malevolent pain that made me want to throw up and pass out at the same time. I mean, I was sweating, crying, and moaning on my knees beside the bed, "Lord, just take me now!"

My friend took me to the Emergency Room. The doctor said, "*Not much we can do about this. You'll just have to wait until they pass through.*"

"Pass through?!", I said, "I'm dyin' here!"

So, the doctor prescribed codeine and gave me a few until I could get to the pharmacy. *"Don't take these until you get home and in bed,"* he told me.

I wanted to pop one right there!

But I waited. Good thing, too.

I had never had anything stronger than aspirin before the moment I took that *first* codeine.

If you've never had codeine or something like it, it is nearly impossible for you to understand what happened a few minutes later, but I'll try to describe it the best I can.

I took that first codeine and, there I was lying in bed in the fetal position, moaning and groaning like a distempered baby. I didn't know if I was going to make it.

All I could think about was the pain. The pain.

Then a few minutes later, the pain started to lessen, and then it was gone! Totally gone! It was a miracle of modern-day medicine! I was pain free, just like that!

But that wasn't all (and if you've had codeine or morphine you know what I'm talking about), not only was the pain gone, but so was anxiety, fear, negativity, that constant hum of "what am I supposed to do now", they were all gone!

I was at total peace with myself and the world. Everything was right and good with the world.

Never had I felt this way before. All that baggage that I had just gotten "used to" was simply *gone*.

That day, I literally just sat there in bed and watched the sunspot coming through the window move along the wall until it was evening. And as far as I was concerned, that was a *perfectly good* use of my time!

I felt no compulsion to get *anything* "done", no anxiety about wasting my time, no misgivings about not going to work. I was perfectly content just... being.

Now, the addiction part is probably easy to imagine, even if you've never had codeine.

Imagine...a tiny little pill ends all your problems and ushers you into a world filled with happiness, contentment, rainbows and unicorns, and you don't have to do anything but just... be.

Avoiding Abuse

Fortunately, the kidney stones passed the next day, and I didn't *need* the codeine anymore...whew!

But I kept taking it on Day 2. Well, I had a bunch left...why waste them, right? I was becoming addicted to codeine.

By then, I was taking several codeines a day! [To this day I still have no idea why the doctor prescribed so many.]

The normal "baggage" had come back in spades, and by my accounting had brought some malicious friends with it.

The anxiety was back. The fear was back.

I need to get back to work and do something productive. I must do something to get back to Happy World. Take a codeine, man, no one will blame you. You've been through a lot. Just take one more.

It was always *just one more.*

On Day 3, I woke up knowing that I had just spent the last 2 days in a fake world, a world where I could not get better, and could not function.

None of it was real. I needed to do something drastic to end the cycles. I had to take a stand and NOW.

I went into the bathroom, and without allowing myself to think about the "baggage" and its friends, I grabbed the remaining codeine and flushed them all down the toilet.

I called the doctor and told him what I did. He said that was a good thing.

When to Stop

I had a friend when I was younger who got into a bad accident. The doctors gave him codeine for the pain. He got hooked and it messed him up pretty badly.

So, if you're on codeine or something similar, let me give you some heart-felt advice. Stop as soon as you can.

The moment most of the pain is gone, dump the pain killers.

Or as soon as you start taking them, not to end unbearable pain, but just to feel "good", I recommend that you dump the pills.

Do NOT think, "I'm OK, I'll stop when they run out."

Wrong-O.

No, what you'll do is call the doctor and tell him about the pain that you're in (which you're not) and how you need a refill (which you don't).

I felt these things and I thought these things.

The way to end the possibility of addiction is to flush those puppies down the toilet the second you, or some else, realizes you're taking them to feel "normal." Just sayin'.

CHAPTER 8

FINANCES

Don't Get Stressed Out, It's Gonna Be OK

Amputation surgery and the associated hospitalization, and follow-up visits can be *expensive* and unless you have a boatload of money or fantastic health insurance, you're going to be paying a good chunk of those costs out-of-pocket. This can be some cause for concern.

But chill out. Don't worry about it. You're gonna be alright. For one thing most medical providers, especially at this crazy time (September 2020), are happy to get *anything* from patients.

Most are quite happy to negotiate a payment plan with you. Some will even negotiate fees.

I had to deal with this because my insurance plan through my employer wasn't particularly good. It didn't cover much. So, I had a night or two of anxiety. But I looked for and found some solutions. I want to share them with you.

In this chapter, I explain what the various documents are, and share with you the tools and strategies I learned and used to deal with these bills.

Bills

Depending on who your health insurance provider is, and how the health provider bills, you might receive their bill first or the insurance provider's *Explanation of Benefits* (EOB) first.

If you receive the bill first, hang on and wait for the EOB. Make sure that the health provider's billing department has your correct, current insurance information, not a previous one.

Understanding the "Explanation of Benefits"

The **Explanation of Benefits** (EOB) comes from your insurance company after your health care provider submits their bills to the insurance company. The EOB basically enumerates the procedures they were charged for, the costs they were charged, what they paid, and what they didn't pay for.

A Strategy to Deal with Medical Bills

Dealing with the medical bills and EOBs that can pile up after a major surgery can be daunting, but with the right strategy, tools, and no small amount of hutzpah, you can get through it relatively unscathed.

The whole process is all about *organization, people skills, patience, persistence,* and *proactiveness.*

Here's another great moment to brag on my amazing wife, Jackie. Jackie is the grand master of people skills. She was also a patient care coordinator for a remarkably busy doctor's office for years, so she has the skills, you know? Jackie coached me through a good chuck of this process, and I owe her big time.

Here are some helpful ideas to help you weather the storm, and possibly even enjoy it. (OK, perhaps that's a stretch.)

Be Organized

Between the Explanation of Benefits (EOB), the bills, the various insurance forms, and whatnot, this whole thing can get a bit confusing and even scary. So being organized *really* helps.

What I did was have a folder with sections and kept everything in there, nicely organized.

One of the trickiest parts of dealing with medical bills is matching up the EOB and the bills. Not understanding what the EOB is and how it relates to your bills can end up costing you a lot of money.

Not knowing how to deal with bills can end up costing you a lot of money.

What I did was to put all the information into a spreadsheet.

This makes filtering, sorting, finding things, and synchronizing the data from the EOB and the bills from my health care providers much easier. This makes understanding what's going on and what I need to do much easier and clearer.

Here are the columns that I used in the spreadsheet:

- **Date** (of treatment)
- **Insurance Company** (if you have more than one – I did)

- **Claim ID** (Insurance company)
- **Insurance Description** (of treatment)
- **Code** (from provider – this is the standardized medical code)
- **Provider Description** (from bill)
- **Amount Charged**
- **Amount Covered** (by insurance)
- **Amount Not Covered** (that I must pay)
- **Explanation** [Covered, ShouldCover, Investigate, Negotiate] (We'll cover these soon)
- **Action** [Confirm, Negotiate, Fight] (We'll cover what these are soon)
- **Notes** (anything that helps I deal with this charge)

My strategy was as follows:

1. **Gather** all relevant information (EOB, bills, contact information, notes)
2. **Organize** the information (in a spreadsheet and a folder)
3. If any information is missing, call the provider or insurance to get it.
4. Get a copy of your **medical records** from all providers you dealt with during the entire process.

5. Get a copy of your medical insurance **coverage policy**(ies).

6. **Study** and mark your policy(ies) with a highlighter the areas relevant to your situation.

7. Make sure you **understand** your coverage in these areas, and if you don't, call the company to get clarity.

8. As EOBs and bills come in, add them to the **spreadsheet** and sync up the data. Your goal is to have all the columns filled in and have no duplicate rows.

9. **Communicate** any questions or concerns you have with the provider or insurance company.

10. **Track** any communications with the providers (Date and time, Organization, Name of person, what the call was about, action items). Track official or legal communications in writing and used registered mail.

11. **Apply** for any financial aid programs available from the providers, the State, or federally. Sometimes you can use these to defray some of the costs.

12. **Wait** until all the bills have been run through all insurance programs. Don't pay anything unless you already agreed to so do.

13. **Clarify** with the insurance company why they didn't cover a charge when the policy seems to say it should. Get this in writing.

14. Once you're sure that the insurance has covered everything it should, then **reassess** that amount that you need to cover. Make sure you are totally clear on these charges.

15. At this phase, begin to **negotiate** with the providers on the remaining amounts. Negotiate on price and a payment plan.

16. Once you get agreement, **pay** according to the plan as agreed. Be sure to use **financial aid** resources that are available and that you could qualify for.

In my case, after getting some very expensive bills, I investigated on my employer's benefits website and found out that I had a *secondary health insurance plan a hospitalization cost protection plan*.

So, I called the insurance company and got my ID and Group numbers.

Then I called all of the providers that sent me bills and gave them the new insurance information and politely asked them to run the bills through the second insurance company.

Not only did this just buy me another few weeks, but the secondary plan is specifically for the types of charges the bills enumerated, so these charges were covered, at least in part, by the secondary insurance company.

Be Polite

The whole medical thing can be mystifying, confusing, and stressful.

And not just for you, but also for the nice folks at the provider's offices and the insurance company. They're just trying to do their jobs, so be kind and courteous.

Being polite and direct with those you contact. Be clear, respectful and concise about what you need from them.

Be patient because sometimes it can take a while to get to the right computer screen or find the right information.

Write down their names and call them by name. Everyone likes to hear the sound of their names.

Keep notes about calls and emails. Include the name of the person you're working with, the date and time of the call, the substance of the call, and any questions asked or answered.

These notes are critical if you must negotiate with a provider or insurance company, or if litigation is required (more on that later).

Be Proactive

Do *not* wait until you receive all the EOBs or bills.

Start right away, even *before* you get anything. Contact your insurance company(ies) and get copies of my policy(ies).

Request copies of your medical records right way.

And as soon as you receive an EOB or bill, add the data to spreadsheet.

Be Persistent

It might take a few rounds with the insurance company to get everything covered that should be covered by the policy.

Be persistent. Keep resubmitting requests.

Negotiate

Suffice it to say that I am not a natural-born negotiator. In fact, I stink at it.

My amazing wife, Jackie, is awesome at negotiating.

So, I not only had her help me to learn negotiation, but Jackie stepped in and handled most of the negotiating. I just sat back in awe and watched the show.

Resources to Help Deal with Medical Bills

Amputee Coalition

One of the best resources I have seen is the Amputee Coalition. This site has oodles of great resources, among them a very long list of organizations (https://www.amputee-coalition.org/resources/financial-assistance-for-prosthetic-services/) that might be able to help with various costs associated with medical care.

Be Your Own Advocate

Sometimes the best way to lower costs is to deal directly with the insurance company and the medical provider. But you must do it right.

A great resource for this is the book "**Insurance Coverage & Reimbursement**" (https://shop.amputee-coalition.org/insurance-coverage--reimbursement-p5.aspx).

It can be found on the Amputee Coalition site. This book helped me form the basis of my technique to handle this process.

CONCLUSION

Well this *has* been, and *still* is, an amazing journey in life.

I am astonished at the incredible faith and strength of my amazing wife, Jackie, and the resilience of our kiddos, Michael, and Alyssa.

I'm also blown away and very grateful for the incredible love, care, and generosity of dear friends and relatives who have lavishly given to my GoFundMe campaign, sent us checks, helped with errands, prepared and delivered meals, sent us GrubHub and DoorDash gift cards, consistently prayed for me and my family, and supported me while I worked my way through this challenge.

Indeed this has been a journey that has strengthened me physically, mentally, emotionally, and spiritually.

The bottom line is that I really *couldn't* have done it without the LORD, without my wife and children, without my extended family, our friends, and many others who were there when I needed them.

I'm *still* in process, ultimately, we all are.

I hope that you've found my story interesting and inspiring. And I hope that the information I shared was helpful to you, whether you are an amputee, a caregiver, a family member, or a friend.

Whoever you are, whatever role you're playing in the story, or wherever you are in the story, I hope that this has helped you gain insight, understanding, hope, encouragement, and I hope you laughed a bit... because life is joyful, even if you, or a loved one, has been thrown a curveball.

My hope is that this book will help you get your stance at the plate, keep your eye on that curveball, and knock that sucker out of the park!

L→R: Alyssa, Jim, Jackie, and Michael –
with Jim's favorite painting.
Remember: You are the lion!

APPENDIX
RESOURCES

Mission Gait's YouTube Channel
https://www.youtube.com/c/MissionGait/videos

Mission Gate is created by physical therapists, and this YouTube channel has a ton of useful videos for amputees, their families, and caregivers.

They specialize in gait training, an important part of regaining efficient mobility.

Footless Jo's YouTube Channel
(https://www.youtube.com/channel/UCvFroKGv BjvALxCTFzZXL5w)

A fellow amputee with lots of stories and tips. Jo's channel is where I first heard of the iWalk.

Amputee Coalition

Amputee Coalition's website:
https://www.amputee-coalition.org/

This is the best website I've seen for amputee resources with numerous resources and connections:
https://www.amputee-coalition.org/limb-loss-resource-center/resources-filtered/

There are many ways to become involved and help other amputees. The Amputee Coalition also has a very long list of links to organizations that might be able to help with finances as well.
https://www.amputee-coalition.org/resources/financial-assistance-for-prosthetic-services/

They have a page of links to places where I can donate or exchange unneeded shoes
https://www.amputee-coalition.org/resources/shoe-exchanges/

iWalkFree [https://amzn.to/2LtGiyg]

https://iwalk-free.com/

This is the manufacturer of the iWalk 2.0 that I've raved about.

The site has instructional videos on how to put it together, fit it, and how use the iWalk.

They also have a great webpage just for BKA amputees: https://iwalk-free.com/below-knee-amputation/

They even have a testimonial video from Harrison Ford and other celebrities: https://iwalk-free.com/testimonials/#celeb

And they sell spare parts and replacement parts: https://store.iwalk-free.com/collections/spare-parts

Dr. Livingood

https://drlivingood.com/

Dr. Livingood is a great resource for health and his natural approach to overall heath is exceptional. Both my wife and I have been on his program, and we've used many of his products with great success.

Jim and his Family

Alyssa, Jackie, Jim, Michael at their favorite coffeehouse. Their children haven't tried the delicious coffee yet...instead they've enjoyed their hot chocolate and their desserts.

Christmas Day 2020
Jim and Jackie, Michael and Alyssa

JAMES R. MOREY

Jim Morey is a Software Engineer, Technology Consultant and a multiple-time #1 Bestselling Author. He is a top-rated Udemy Course Creator and a nationally recognized Book Writing and Publishing Coach.

Jim worked at Microsoft for over 18 years in server and Internet technologies including IIS, Operations Manager, SharePoint, and Azure, has written over 250K lines of code in C#, VB, javaScript, PowerShell, and has worked heavily in HTML5, CSS, T-SQL. Over the last seven years, he created several end-to-end marketing platforms.

Aside from these, he has also focused his humor and resources to overcome the challenges of a below the knee amputation and also help others overcome these challenges.

Jim thoroughly enjoys traveling, bicycle riding, cooking, savoring delicious food from many different cultures, and is on a Keto-lifestyle. Most of all, he's a blessed Husband and a proud Dad of their two kids.

PLEASE RATE MY BOOK

I would be honored if you would please take a few moments to rate my book on Amazon.com (U.S.).

Or, if you're in any of these countries, please use these Amazon sites:

Amazon.ca (Canada)
Amazon.co.uk (U.K.)
Amazon.com.au (Australia)
Amazon.fr (France)

Amazon.de (Germany)
Amazon.co.jp (Japan)
Amazon.com.mx (Mexico)
Amazon.es (Spain)

A 5-star rating *and* a short review (e.g. "Very helpful!" or "Excellent resource!") would be much appreciated. I welcome longer, positive comments as well.

If you feel like this book should be rated at three stars or fewer, please hold off posting your comments on Amazon. Instead, please send your feedback directly to my wife and publisher – Jackie, so that we can use it to improve the next edition. We're committed to providing the best value to our customers and readers, and your thoughts can make that possible.

You can reach Jackie or me at CustomerStrategyAcademy@gmail.com.

Thank you very much!

To your success and prosperity with a purpose,

Jim Morey

Multiple-time #1 Bestselling Author
CustomerStrategyAcademy@gmail.com

Printed in Great Britain
by Amazon

17912356R00080